Progressive
GUITAR MASTERPIECES
OF THE
19th CENTURY

Edited by
Jason Waldron

60 MINUTE STEREO CASSETTE AVAILABLE

All the pieces in Progressive Guitar Masterpieces of the Nineteenth Century have been recorded on to a 60 minute STEREO cassette tape.

Cassettes available from all good music stores or direct from

U.S.A. - $9.99 (Ca. residents add tax)
Koala Publications Inc.
3001 Redhill Ave.
Bldg. 2 # 221
Costa Mesa
CA. 92626
Ph. (714) 546 2743

U.K - Music Land £5.95
(includes V.A.T.)
9 St. Petersgate,
Stockport.
Chesire SK1 1EB
Ph (061) 474 7104

AUSTRALIA - $13.99
Koala Publications
P.O. Box 140
Burnside
South Australia 5066
Ph (08) 268 1750

If ordering direct please add $1.00 or 50p. postage per item. Payment by cheque or money order

Acknowledgements

Cover design by David Summerhays

Distributed By

in **Australia**
Koala Publications
P.O. Box 140, Burnside 5066
Ph (08) 268 1750
Fax (08) 352 4760

in **U.S.A.**
Koala Publications
P.O. Box 27, Santa Ana
CA 92702 USA
Ph (714) 546 2743
Fax (714) 546 2749

in **U.K. and Europe**
Music Exchange
Unit 2, Ringway Trading Estate,
Shadow Moss Road, Wythenshawe,
Manchester M226LX
Ph (061) 436 5110
Fax (061) 443 1379

ISBN 0 947183 19 1

List of Contents

KEY

No. 1	Study	Fernando Sor (1788 - 1839)	
No. 2	Study	F. Sor	
No. 3	Study	F. Sor	
No. 4	Study	Dionisio Aguado (1784 - 1849)	
No. 5	Study in Octaves	D. Aguado	
No. 6	Waltz	Mauro Giuliani (1781 - 1829)	
No. 7	Allegretto	Joseff Kuffner (19th C.)	C maj
No. 8	Allegretto	M. Giuliani	
No. 9	Study	D. Aguado	
No. 10	Maestoso	M. Giuliani	
No. 11	Andantino	Matteo Carcassi (1792 - 1853)	
No. 12	Study	Napoleon Coste (1806 - 1883)	
No. 13	Andantino	M. Giuliani	
No. 14	Andante	F. Sor	
No. 15	Andante	Manuel Cano (19th C.)	
No. 16	Study	D. Aguado	
No. 17	Study	D. Aguado	
No. 18	Study	M. Giuliani	
No. 19	Study	D. Aguado	
No. 20	Andantino	Felix Horetzky (19th C.)	
No. 21	Study	M. Carcassi	A min
No. 22	Study	D. Aguado	
No. 23	Allegretto	M. Giuliani	
No. 24	Andante	F. Sor	
No. 25	Agitato	M. Giuliani	
No. 26	Larghetto	F. Sor	
No. 27	Study	D. Aguado	
No. 28	Study	F. Carulli (1770 - 1841)	
No. 29	Scherzo	Anton Diabelli (1781 - 1858)	
No. 30	Study	D. Aguado	
No. 31	Study	D. Aguado	G maj
No. 32	Allegretto	M. Giuliani	
No. 33	Andantino	M. Giuliani	
No. 34	Andante	F. Sor	
No. 35	Andantino	M. Giuliani	
No. 36	Study	D. Aguado	
No. 37	Study	D. Aguado	
No. 38	Study	M. Carcassi	
No. 39	Andante	F. Sor	E min
No. 40	Study	D. Aguado	
No. 41	Study	F. Sor	
No. 42	Mazurca	Rocamora (19th C.)	
No. 43	Study	M. Carcassi	
No. 44	Study	A. Diabelli	
No. 45	Allegro	M. Giuliani	D maj
No. 46	Andantino	F. Carulli	
No. 47	Andantino	M. Giuliani	
No. 48	Study	F. Sor	B min
No. 49	Study	M. Cano	
No. 50	Study	D. Aguado	A maj
No. 51	Study	F. Sor	
No. 52	Lesson	D. Aguado	
No. 53	Andante	F. Carulli	F maj
No. 54	Allegretto	M. Giuliani	
No. 55	Allegro	M. Giuliani	D min
No. 56	Andantino	M. Giuliani	

Guitar Masterpieces of the 19th Century

Arranged by Jason Waldron

Foreward

Progressive Guitar Masterpieces of the 19th Century is essential for all beginning guitarists to establish a strong technique and to gain a knowledge of the Classical Period.

All pieces are carefully graded and are in logical progression in terms of the major and minor keys common to the guitar. This will help to develop the students ear and sight-reading capabilities.

It is suitable to use as a supplement for all guitar methods, but is specifically designed to be used in conjunction with the very successful "Progressive Classical Guitar" by Jason Waldron.

For further study, the series of "Popular Classics of the Great Composers" (featuring the music of Beethoven, Brahms, Chopin, Schubert etc., arranged for the classical guitarist by Jason Waldron) are invaluable.

TECHNICAL NOTE:

1. Fingering is included for all pieces only once and not again for repeated passages.

2. Dynamics and tempo markings have been ommitted to allow the player to use his/her own ideas based on the general "feel" of the music.

Fernando Sor (b. Barcelona 1778 - d. Paris 1839)

Perhaps the greatest of all the classical period guitar personalities, Sor began study of the violin and cello before receiving a thorough education in harmony and composition at the famous monastery of Montserrat near Barcelona.

After discovering the guitar, Sor discarded his early instruments in its favour and soon reached such a high level of proficiency that he amazed all who heard him.

Sor visited Madrid and received a commision to write music for both the Duchess of Alba and the Duke of Medina.

During the war with Portugal, Sor joined the Spanish Army, serving as a Captain. He was later expelled to France where he stayed until his move in 1809 to London.

He had such great success in London that he decided to settle there to teach and compose; it was here that the majority of his 400 works for guitar were composed.

Sor wrote a fine Method and his compositions which include Studies, Waltzes, Minuets and Themes with variations confirm the French critic Fetis' statement that Sor was the "Beethoven of the Guitar."

PLAYING NOTES: These 3 studies are essentially single line and a lot of importance should be placed on the fingering for both hands especially the alternation of right hand fingering as well as a steady tempo - count the beats before attempting to play.

No. 1 — Study — Fernando Sor (1778-1839)

No. 2 — Study — F. Sor

No. 3   Study   F. Sor

No. 4   # Study   **Dionisio Aguado (1784 - 1849)**

PLAYING NOTES: This piece is in two distinct parts or voices, so each part must be practised separately whilst either counting or saying the names of the notes.

No. 5   # Study in Octaves   **D. Aguado**

PLAYING NOTES: An excellent study to consolidate common fingerings in the 1st position N.B. repeat signs.

No. 6   Waltz   Mauro Giuliani (1781 - 1829)

PLAYING NOTES: Special notice should be taken of the quarter and eighth note rests - particularly in the bass. This can most easily be obtained by resting the thumb (p) on the string when necessary to dampen the note.

No. 7   Allegretto   Joseff Kuffner (19th C.)

PLAYING NOTES: Be sure to observe the "accidentals" (sharps, flats and naturals) and the tied notes in the bass (Bars 3 & 4 and 19 & 20). Retain a legato (smooth) arpeggio.

No. 8   Allegretto

M. Giuliani

PLAYING NOTES: This piece is an excellent combination of chords, arpeggios and single line playing. Take particular notice of the timing changes (Bar 17 triplets and Bar 25 sixteenth notes). As with all pieces play strongly and count the beats in each bar.

Dionisio Aguado (b. Madrid 1784 - d. Madrid 1849)

Aguado was taught the elements of music and guitar by the monk Basilio in Madrid and later received more advanced tuition by the renowned singer and guitarist, Manuel Garcia.

Retiring to his estate near Aranjuez during the French invasion, he dedicated his time to writing his famous Method which was published in Madrid in 1825.

Aguados' brilliant technique is only equalled by his good taste in composition which epitomize all of his works for guitar.

Living in Paris from 1825, Aguado met and formed a lasting friendship with Fernando Sor with whom he shared teaching rooms and performed duets.

An indication of Aguados' amiable personality is shown in the story of his capture for ransom by Spanish banditos late in his life. Apparently the old man was so charming that these hardened men were won over and released him unharmed and free of ransom payment.

No. 9	Study	D. Aguado

PLAYING NOTES: In this piece the right hand arpeggios change between ④ ③ & ② using i m & a to ③ ②
& ① so be sure to move the right hand to accomodate this.

No. 10   **Maestoso**   **M. Giuliani**

PLAYING NOTES: Study 10 is in two distinct voices and each must be practised separately. Be sure to observe all the accidentals and fingering.

Matteo Carcassi (b. Florence 1792 - d. Paris 1853)

Carcassi, a brilliant virtuoso, arrived in Paris in 1820 where he soon displaced the aged Carulli as premier performer and composer for guitar.

Using Paris as a base, he made numerous trips to London where he was received enthusiastically by a guitar hungry audience.

His method (which is one of the most popular ever written) has assured his place in the guitars' didactic literature, as have his many compositions, all of which are of great technical merit and musical charm.

No. 11   # Andantino   **Matteo Carcassi (1792-1853)**

PLAYING NOTES: Concentrate on strength, evenness and smooth left hand changes in the second section - i.e. do not push hand away when using the 3rd finger in bar 8.

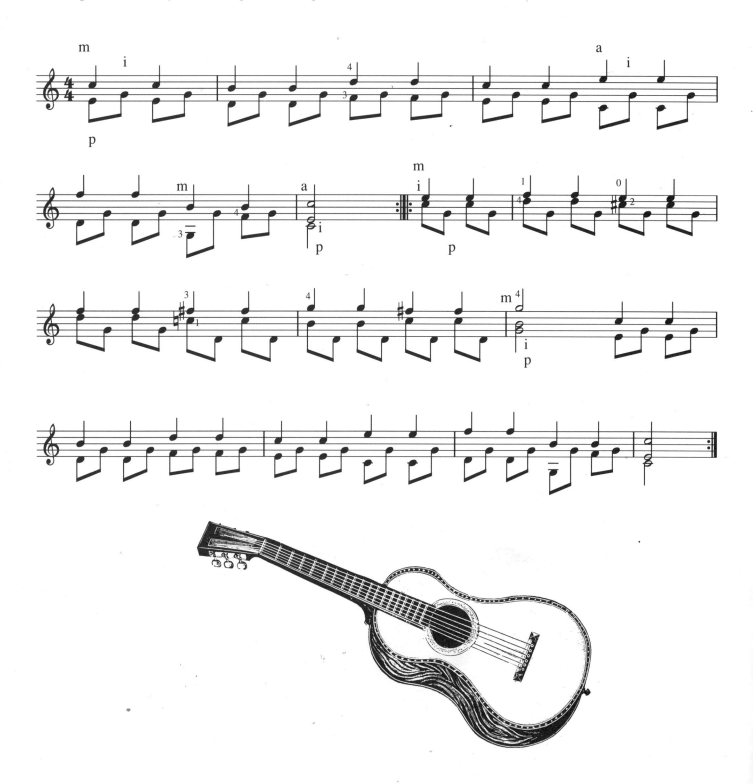

Napoleon Coste (1806 -1883)

Born in Daubs in 1806, Coste began his study of the guitar at the age of six and by eighteen was teaching in Valencienne. He moved to Paris in 1830 where he was highly praised as a concert artist and teacher by the musical press and his friends Sor, Carulli, Aguado and Carcassi.

The breaking of his arm, and consequent loss of technical ability in 1840 led to his concetration on composition and the publication of his works.

He lived primarily in Paris until his death in 1883.

PLAYING NOTES: These 3 pieces are good examples of two part writing and each voice should be practiced separately. Note the use of the open G or 3rd string as a continuous "pedal" which holds the pieces together harmonically. This is a very common technique used by guitar composers of the classical period.

No. 12   **Study**   Napoleon Coste (1806 - 1883)

No. 13

Andantino

M. Giuliani

No. 14　　　　　　**Andante**　　　　　　F. Sor

PLAYING NOTES: The new key of A minor is very well suited to the guitar as it uses the chords of Am, Dm and E7, all of which have bass notes on an open string (Am ⑤, Dm ④ and E7 ⑥). Be very aware of the G sharps and make sure to play the chords "together" in Study 16.

No. 15 — Andante — Manuel Cano (19th C.)

No. 16 — Study — D. Aguado

No. 17   Study   D. Aguado

PLAYING NOTES: This arpeggio study can be played using a variety of right hand combinations for example, p m a m, p i a i, or by changing the orders of the notes p m i m, p a m a, etc.

PLAYING NOTES: As in most of the following pieces, Studies 18 & 19 "modulate" into the relative major key before returning to the minor - in this case Am, C, Am. This change to the relative major gives a temporary "happy" feel to the otherwise somber minor mood.

No. 18   Study   M. Giuliani

No. 19   Study   D. Aguado

No. 20   Andantino   Felix Horetzky (19th C.)

PLAYING NOTES: Study no. 20 is in the style of the Italian "Sisciliana" and should be played with a lilting rhythm. It has many interesting features, not the least of which are the many accidentals (sharps, flats and naturals). Remember that an accidental only applies to the bar in which it occurs therefore the B♭ accidental in bar 10 is automatically returned to B♮ in bar 12.

PLAYING NOTES: Two excellent arpeggio studies which should be practiced strongly and evenly with careful attention to fingering. As in Study 17, Study 22 can use different right hand combinations.

No. 21   # Study   **M. Carcassi**

No. 22   Study   D. Aguado

No. 23   **Allegretto**   M. Giuliani

PLAYING NOTES: Keep a steady rhythm and make sure to use the fingering as indicated.

No. 24   Andante   F. Sor

PLAYING NOTES: This study has many timing changes so count through before attempting to play. At "Fine" it changes key to the relative major, C, and at the sign 𝄋 returns to the minor key to finish.

No. 25   Agitato   M. Giuliani

PLAYING NOTES: As its title indicates this study has a rather agitated feel caused by the *"syncopated" rhythm.
Be sure to obey the "ties" at the end of bars 8 & 42.
    * See Progressive Classical Guitar Method pg. 81

No. 26   Larghetto   F. Sor

PLAYING NOTES: This beautiful piece must be played majestically and with special attention to the dotted eighth notes, i.e. bar 1.

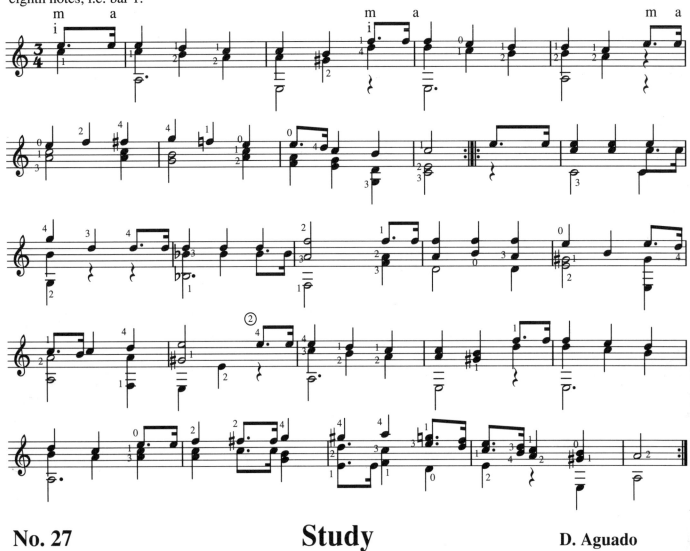

No. 27   **Study**   D. Aguado

PLAYING NOTES: In the new key G major all F notes are played as F sharps as indicated by the "key signature". In Study 27 make sure to play the notes on the correct strings as indicated by the number in a circle. - i.e. ③ means to play the note on the 3rd strings.

Ferdinand Carulli (b. Naples 1770 - d. Paris 1841)

Carulli, who's method op. 241 is still widely used today, is mainly remembered for his excellent studies, especially those for beginners.

He also wrote much music for guitar and ensemble including trios for guitar, flute and violin, trios for three guitars, and duos for two guitars and guitar and piano.

Carulli wrote several Concerti for guitar and small orchestra (which are seldom heard today) as well as his "Harmony applied to the Guitar" which examines the art of accompaniment.

No. 28 **Study** **Ferdinand Carulli (1770-1841)**

No. 29   Scherzo   Anton Diabelli (1781-1858)

PLAYING NOTES: Study 29 is entitled "Scherzo" which means joke, it should be played with humour and special attention given to the rests which often occur, completely stopping all sound for one and sometimes two quarter beats.

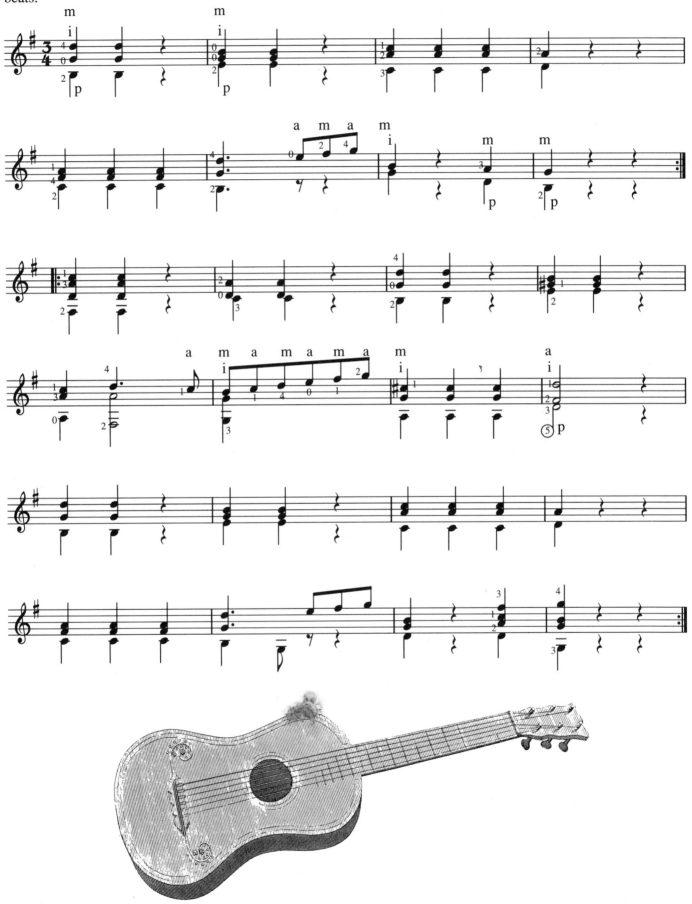

No. 30   Study   D. Aguado

PLAYING NOTES:In the first section a group of arpeggios are followed by a block chord which must be played cleanly and without any broken sound. In bar 9 the G sharp accidental is used throughout the bar.

No. 31   Study   D. Aguado

PLAYING NOTES: Study 31 is in two voices and therefore each should be practised separately. As always count the beats and say the names of the notes.

Mauro Giuliani (b. Barletta 1781 - d. Vienna 1829)

A self taught guitarist like most of the players in the late eighteenth and early nineteenth centuries, Giulianis' brilliant playing inspired Beethoven to comment "the guitar is a miniature orchestra in itself".

    Giuliani lived in Vienna from 1807 to 1821 where he was appointed chamber musician and teacher to the Archduchess Marie Louise and counted such great musicians as Moscheles, Hummel and Diabelli as his friends.

    His works range from easy teaching pieces (including the famous "Papillion" op. 30) to very demanding works of the highest quality; much of it written in the Italian style of his great contemporary Rossini.

    Giulianis' duets for two guitars, guitar and violin and guitar and flute are amongst the finest ever written as is his magnificent "Concerto for guitar and small orchestra op. 30".

PLAYING NOTES: Both of these studies utilize low bass harmonies which must be played very clearly. Be sure to obey all right hand & left hand fingerings.

No. 32   Allegretto   M. Giuliani

No. 33   Andantino

M. Giuliani

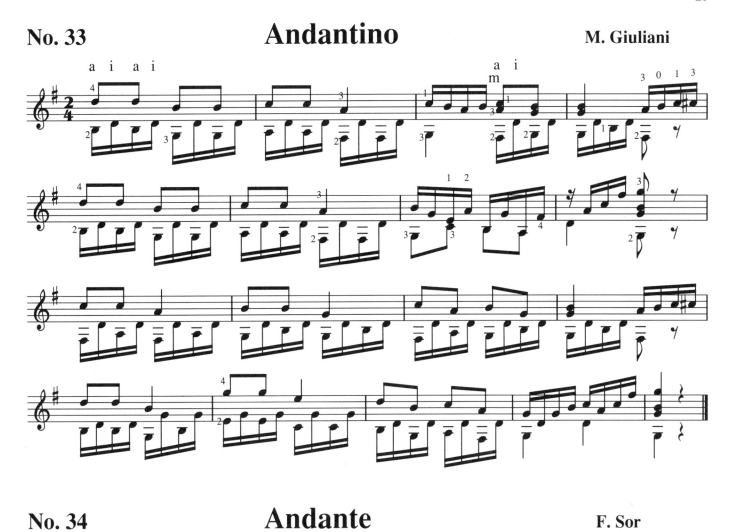

No. 34   Andante

F. Sor

PLAYING NOTES: Play this study gracefully and pay carefull attention to " legato" or smoothness. Note the "chromatic" voice at bars 9, through to 13.

No. 35   Andantino   M. Giuliani

PLAYING NOTES: Study 35 involves most of the techniques used in the previous G major studies as well as a "question and answer" effect in the top line followed by the bass line e.g. bars 1 & 2. Make sure to "alternate" right hand fingers.

No. 36   Study   D. Aguado

PLAYING NOTES: The new key of E minor is also very well suited to the guitar due to the use of the chords Em and Am both of which have open basses, Em ⑥ & Am ⑤ . B7 is the 3rd chord or "Dominant 7th". In Study 36 be sure to clearly dot the eighth notes as indicated.

No. 37   Study   D. Aguado

PLAYING NOTES: Play each chord in this study "together" & strongly. It is very good practice in the "spreading" of the right hand fingers , i.e. in the first chord, a plucks ① , m plucks ③ and i plucks ④ therefore leaving ② clear.

No. 38   Study   M. Carcassi

PLAYING NOTES: Play this study slowly, making sure to make all the chord changes clean and distinct. The scale at bar 15 should be practiced using both free stroke and rest stroke.

No. 39   Andante   F. Sor

PLAYING NOTES: Study 39 incorporates repeats and 1st and 2nd time endings (see Progressive Classical Guitar Method pg. 42). Left hand fingerings are extremelly important as is the "tie" at the end of bar 21.

No. 40   Study   D. Aguado

PLAYING NOTES: This study introduces the important right hand arpeggio p i m a m i which, when mastered at a high speed is very effective. To accomodate speed, "grip" p i m a at the beginning of each group and "peel off" the fingers one at a time keeping each finger movement as small as possible. N.B. Accidentals occur quite often and these must be observed for the whole bar.

No. 41 Study F. Sor

PLAYING NOTES: Use rest strokes on the top line of this study and make the left hand changes as smooth as possible.

No. 42   Mazurka   Rocamora (19th C.)

PLAYING NOTES: Study 42 is a "Mazurka" or the Polish variant of the waltz which uses a dotted rhythm as in the second section of this study. It is another good example of the key change from Em to G then finishing on Em.

No. 43   Study   M. Carcassi

PLAYING NOTES: The new key of D includes a C sharp in the key signature as well as retaining the F sharp from the previous keys G & Em. Study 43 provides good practice in holding down one finger-in this case 4 and moving the other fingers around it. Keep the left hand steady and do not arch the wrist too greatly.

No. 44   Study   A. Diabelli

PLAYING NOTES: Note the use of the "pedal bass" in this study - D notes in the first section and A and D notes in the second section. Keep the right hand very steady and move the right hand thumb in a circular motion (see Progressive Classical Guitar Method pg. 22), very independant of the fingers.

No. 45　Allegro　M. Giuliani

PLAYING NOTES: This study is marked Allegro but as with all pieces practice them slowly at first until completely sure of the timing, fingering etc. Note the quarter note rests in the bass line - these can most easily be achieved by resting the thumb on the string.

PLAYING NOTES: Pay special attention to the timing of Studies 46 & 47 as both include the use of quarter, eighth & sixteenth notes. In particular, Study 47 has a group of triplets (see Progressive Classical Guitar Method pg. 57) from bar 21 to the end of bar 24 before returning to sixteenth notes.

No. 46   **Andantino**   F. Carulli

No. 47   Andantino

M. Giuliani

No. 48   Study   F. Sor

PLAYING NOTES: This Study is in B minor, the relative minor to D major. Be sure to alternate the right hand fingers and observe left hand fingering positions, accidentals etc.

D.C. al Fine

PLAYING NOTES: The key of A includes a new sharp, G sharp along with that of F sharp and C sharp.
  Studies 49 and 50 are similar in structure but whereas Study 49 must be played very legato, Study 50 has more of a "hopping" feel due to the dotted eighth notes.

No. 49 # Study **M. Cano**

No. 50 # Study **D. Aguado**

No. 51   Study   F. Sor

PLAYING NOTES: Study 51 must be played extremely smoothly and steady with careful attention given to the left hand chord changes.

No. 52   **Lesson**   D. Aguado

PLAYING NOTES: This Study is in two voices and makes use of both pivot and slide fingers (Progressive Classical Guitar Method pg. 43). It also involves the use of the half bar (Progressive Classical Guitar Method pg. 72) which must be placed correctly in order to accomodate the 4th finger in its stretch to the top note A. Left hand fingering is of particular importance.

No. 53   **Andante**   F. Carulli

PLAYING NOTES: The new key F major includes one flat, B flat, in the key signature. Study 53 is a "Siciliana" as was Study 20. Note that the 3rd section modulates into C major before returning to finish in F.

No. 54   Allegretto   M. Giuliani

PLAYING NOTES: Study 54 is a fairly straight forward scale and arpeggio study but has an interesting technical feature in the 3rd to last bar. To accomodate both the sustain of the top voices (dotted half notes) and the open A note in the bass, the student must lift the tip of the bar finger whilst holding down the three notes on ③② & ① before lowering the bar finger to finish the piece.

No. 55   Allegro   M. Giuliani

PLAYING NOTES: The new key of D minor uses B flat in the key signature and is the relative minor to F major.
      Study 55 is an excellent arpeggio study requiring a clear strong sound, both with the right hand fingers as well as the thumb which plays the melody.

No. 56   **Andantino**   M. Giuliani

PLAYING NOTES: Study 56 uses many of the techniques studied up to now including chords, arpeggios, bars, half bars, pedal notes etc. Special attention should be given to the rests.